Acknowledgements

I would like to thank my mother for fostering a spirit of baking within me.

I would like to thank my husband for supporting my dream to write this cookbook. I would also like to thank my children, family and friends for recipe tasting and all their support.

Special thanks to my friend, Andrine Clarke, who encouraged me to "put pen to paper", as we say, and also for doing the editing and formatting.

Copyright © 2014 2011 by Renaee Smith.
Food Photography © by Renaee Smith
Book and Cover Design by Andrine Clarke

ISBN: Softcover – 978-0-9855415-2-1
Second Edition

All rights reserved. No part of this book may be reproduced or transmitted in any form or by any means, electronic or mechanical, including photocopying, recording, or by any information storage and retrieval system, without permission in writing from the copyright owner.

This book was printed in the United States of America.

To order additional copies of this book, contact:
Renaee Smith
973-723-4584
www.renaeescakes.com

Table of Contents

INTRODUCTION 2

TREATS
Coconut Drops 4
Gizzada 5
Jackass Corn 6
Grater Cake 7
Duckonoo (Tie Leaf or Blue Draws) 8
Peanut Brittle 9

BUNS
Spiced Bun (Easter Bun) 11
Rock Buns 12
Bulla Cake 13
Coconut Toto 14

CAKES
Black Cake (Christmas Cake) 17
Carrot Cake 18

Pineapple Upside-Down Cake 19
Ginger Cake 20
Mango Cake 21
Coffee Cake 23
Pound Cake (Plain Cake) 24
Banana Bread 25

PUDDINGS
Bread Pudding 27
Sweet Potato Pudding 28
Cornmeal Pudding 29

TARTS
Plantain Tart 31
Pineapple Tart 32
Cherry Tart 33

APPENDIX
Metric Charts 34
Index 35

Introduction

My love for baking was sparked at an early age. I remember my mother always "rubbing up something" to put in the oven on a Sunday afternoon after church. The oven was never on without some form of baked treats inside: totos, plain cake and cornmeal pudding with the goodness on top. I have to say, my mom makes the best cornmeal pudding.

My inspiration for this book came from searching for and trying to recreate all those old-time Jamaican snacks that I love. I decided to put them all in one place for other Jamaican cooks and those who like to try different recipes. These recipes are simple and fun. I have tried to keep it authentic and true to Jamaica. However, I have included tips on how to bake them outside of Jamaica using alternate ingredients. Hope you enjoy baking these delicious recipes as much as I do.

Photograph by Andrine Clarke

TREATS

Coconut Drops

I remember my mom asking my dad to cut some banana leaf for the weekend because she was going to make drops. This was a special treat. Nowadays with no banana tree in sight, Reynolds Wrap® will have to do.

Ingredients

1 tbsp ginger
2 cups brown sugar
2 medium-sized dried coconuts chopped to yield 3 cups of coconut
3 cups water
Non-Stick aluminum foil

Directions

1. Break open the coconuts (taste to ensure coconut is fresh).
2. Remove the coconut from the shell.
3. Cut the coconut into small pieces (approx. ⅛ of inch)
4. In a large uncovered pot mix ginger, sugar, coconuts and water.
5. Bring to a rapid boil and reduce the flame to medium high.
6. Allow the mixture to cook until it thickens. Reduce the flame to low. Use a large spoon to continuously stir the mixture to prevent it from burning or sticking to the pot.
7. Cook the mixture until the sugar caramelizes. When the sugar begins to solidify at the bottom of the cooking pot and it is difficult to turn the mixture with the spoon, reduce the flame to the lowest setting.
8. Use a tablespoon to scoop clumps of the mixture onto the Non-Stick aluminum foil.
9. Allow to cool.
10. Yields about 12 coconut drops.

Gizzada

My Auntie Faye used to make the best gizzada. The crust and the filling were the absolute best.

Ingredients for Coconut Filling

1 cup water
1 ½ cups grated coconut
1 tbsp grated ginger
1 ½ cups brown sugar
¼ tsp grated nutmeg
1 oz butter

Ingredients for Crust

2 cups flour
Enough water to make dough
1 tsp shortening
1 tbsp butter
½ tsp salt

Directions for Coconut Filling

1. Boil water and sugar together to make syrup (low heat).
2. Add the grated coconut and nutmeg to the syrup.
3. Stir the ingredients on low heat for 20 minutes so it does not thicken.
4. Add the butter.
5. Stir ingredients for another 5 minutes. Be sure the butter is not visible in the filling.
6. Allow the filling to cool.

Directions for Crust

1. Sift flour and salt together.
2. Cut in butter, shortening and add the cold water (add 1 tbsp at a time) to make dough.
3. Place the dough into a plastic wrapping and refrigerate for 30 minutes.
4. Remove dough from fridge. Flour your surface and then use a rolling pin to roll the dough on a cutting board to a 1/4 inch thickness.
5. Cut circles in the dough using an 8-oz cup/glass or a cookie cutter).
6. Crimp (pinch) each of the circles to form a crust.
7. Place the crusts on a greased tray and bake in oven at 350°F for 15 minutes.
8. Remove from oven and add the filling to each crust.
9. Bake for another 20 minutes.
10. Remove from oven and allow to cool.
11. Yields about 10 depending on size of each gizzada.

Jackass Corn

If you don't have strong teeth you will definitely find out when eating this treat. Slightly sweet with coconut bits throughout.

Ingredients

1 cup flour
¼ tsp baking soda
1 cup sugar
½ tsp nutmeg
½ tsp ginger
¼ tsp salt
1 cup shredded unsweetened coconut
3 tbsp water (or enough to stop the dough from crumbling)

Directions

1. Mix all ingredients
2. Roll out thin and cut into small shapes.
3. Put on greased sheets.
4. Prick with a fork.
5. Bake 8-12 minutes at 375°F (depending on size).
6. Makes 20 – 25.

Grater Cake

Not for the diet conscious as this sweet treat is exactly that ....sweet.

Ingredients

2 cups grated coconut
3 cups sugar
½ cup water
A pinch of salt

Directions

1. Mix all ingredients in a thick bottomed pan.
2. Boil until coconut is cooked and the liquid dries up. The mixture should be sticky enough to hold together.
3. Remove from heat and beat mixture for 2 to 3 minutes.
4. Drop on a greased tray and allow to cool.
5. A second batch can be made and colored pink and placed on top of first batch.
6. Makes about 10 – 12.

Duckonoo (Tie Leaf or Blue Draws)

This was my grandmother's "Mother Dears" cure-all. Whenever someone was sick, you were guaranteed some duckonoo and ginger beer that tickles the back of your throat. I think people would fake a cough just to get a piece of my grandmother's duckonoo. Miss you Mother Dear.

Ingredients

- 3 cups green bananas
- 2 cups sweet potatoes
- 1 cup flour
- 1 tsp baking powder
- 1 tsp salt
- 2 cups coconut milk
- 1 ½ cups brown sugar
- 1 tsp vanilla
- 1 tsp cinnamon
- 2 tbsp melted margarine
- 1 cup grated coconut
- ¼ cup raisins

Directions

1. Combine grated bananas, sweet potatoes, flour, baking powder, salt, cinnamon, margarine, grated coconut and raisins.
2. Combine coconut milk, sugar and vanilla.
3. Pour milk mixture into banana mixture and mix well.
4. Put ½ cup of mixture into banana leaf or foil and fold sides.
5. Tie with twine or banana bark.
6. Place in enough boiling water to cover and boil for 1 hour.
7. Remove from leaf or foil and serve.
8. Yields about 8.

Note: This can be served warm or cold.

Peanut Brittle

This is one of my mom's favorite treats.

Ingredients

1 ½ tsp baking soda
1 tsp water
1 tsp vanilla
1 ½ cups sugar
1 cup water

1 cup light corn syrup
3 tbsp margarine or butter
1 lb raw peanuts
Candy thermometer (optional)

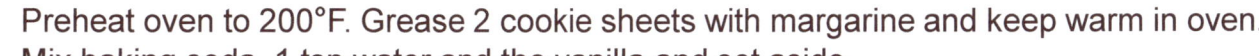

Directions

1. Preheat oven to 200°F. Grease 2 cookie sheets with margarine and keep warm in oven.
2. Mix baking soda, 1 tsp water and the vanilla and set aside
3. Mix sugar, 1 cup water and the corn syrup in a 3-quart saucepan.
4. Cook over medium heat stirring occasionally to 240°F (use a candy thermometer to monitor temperature) or until a small amount of mixture dropped into very cold water forms a soft ball that flattens when removed from water.
5. Stir in margarine and peanuts.
6. Cook, stirring constantly to 300°F or until small amount of mixture dropped into cold water separates into hard, brittle threads.
7. **Immediately** remove from heat.
8. Quickly stir in baking soda mixture until light and foamy.
9. Pour half of the mixture onto a cookie sheet and quickly spread with a buttered spatula about ¼ inch thickness.
10. Cool completely for at least 1 hour. Break into pieces and store in covered container.

BUNS

BUNS

Spiced Bun (Easter Bun

This reminds me of the little rhyme we used to say, "Bun without the cheese is like a kiss without a squeeze".

Ingredients for Spiced Bun

3 ½ cups flour
1 ½ cups sugar
4 tsp baking powder
½ tsp cinnamon
1 tsp nutmeg
A pinch of salt
1 egg (beaten)
2 tbsp melted butter or margarine
2 tsp vanilla
½ tsp rose water
1 cup milk
1 cup raisins, mixed peel, cherries
½ cup cherries

Ingredients for the Glaze

½ cup brown sugar
½ cup water

Directions for Spiced Bun

1. Preheat oven to 300°F.
2. In a large bowl mix together dry ingredients.
3. Mix melted butter, beaten egg, vanilla, rosewater and milk .
4. Pour mixture into dry ingredients and mix well.
5. Add raisins, mixed peels or cherries.
6. Pour into two well greased baking pans.
7. Bake for 1 ¼ hours at 300°F.
8. If desired press a few whole cherries into the top of each bun.

Directions for the Glaze

1. Boil water and sugar until thick.
2. When bun is done pour glaze over the top and return to oven for an additional 8 minutes.

Rock Buns

This is an easy recipe and the first pastry I taught my husband to make.

Ingredients

- 1 cup of flour
- 1 tsp baking powder
- 6 tbsp sugar
- ½ tsp cinnamon
- 6 tbsp butter (frozen)
- ¼ cup shredded coconut
- ½ cup raisins
- 1 egg (beaten)
- ½ tsp vanilla
- Enough milk to make a stiff dough

Directions

1. Preheat oven to 400°F. Grease and flour baking sheet.
2. Mix flour, sugar, cinnamon and baking powder.
3. Cut butter into dry mixture until it looks like fine bread crumbs.
4. Stir in coconut and raisins.
5. Make a hole in center and add beaten egg and vanilla.
6. Add enough milk to mix and make dough stiff.
7. Using a tablespoon, spoon into rough heaps on greased baking sheet.
8. Bake for 15-20 minutes or until golden brown.
9. Yields 12 buns.

Bulla Cake

There's nothing like bulla and pear (avocado)! Great snack, the smooth texture of a ripe pear and the slightly sweet and ginger taste of the bulla is a great combination.

Ingredients

1 ¼ cup very dark sugar
3 cups flour
1 tsp baking powder
½ tsp baking soda
¼ tsp salt
1 tsp cinnamon
¼ tsp nutmeg
½ tsp ground ginger
½ tsp cloves
2 tbsp melted butter or margarine

Directions

1. Preheat oven to 400°F and lightly grease and flour baking sheet
2. Mix sugar with just enough water to make a thick syrup
3. Mix dry ingredients and make a hole in the center
4. Pour syrup and butter into center and mix together. (Do not over mix)
5. Put mixture on a floured surface and knead for 5 minutes.
6. Roll out to a ¼ inch thickness.
7. Cut circles with biscuit cutter.
8. Place bulla on baking sheet and bake for 20 minutes.

Coconut Toto

I've heard that if your cake tasted like a toto it was not a compliment. However, if made right this a wonderful treat.

Ingredients

¼ lb butter
1 cup granulated sugar
2 cups flour
2 tsp baking powder
1 tsp cinnamon
¼ tsp nutmeg
2 cups grated dry coconut
2 tsp vanilla
1 egg (beaten)
½ cup of milk (approximately)

Directions

1. Grease shallow baking tin and preheat oven to 400°F.
2. Cream butter and sugar.
3. Add baking powder, cinnamon and nutmeg to flour.
4. Add coconut.
5. Add flour mixture to butter and sugar mixture.
6. Add vanilla and beaten egg.
7. Add enough milk to make a stiff dough.
8. Spread evenly in greased baking tin.
9. Bake for about 30 minutes or until golden brown.
10. Cut into squares and serve.

CAKES

Black Cake (Christmas Cake)

This is a traditional Christmas cake, as the name suggests, and the fruits are usually soaking for weeks and months in Jamaican rum and or wine. This cake can be made up to 4 weeks in advance as it actually gets better with age.

Ingredients

3 cups soaked fruits
1 lb brown sugar
1 lb butter
9 eggs
1 tbsp vanilla
¼ cup rum
2 tbsp rosewater
2 tsp lime juice
1 tsp lime rind
1 tsp almond flavoring
1 lb flour
4 tsp baking powder
2 tsp cinnamon
2 tsp nutmeg
¼ tsp salt
8-9 tbsp browning

Directions

1. Preheat oven to 350°F, grease and line pan with wax paper.
2. Cream butter and sugar until light and fluffy.
3. Add eggs one at a time and beat well.
4. Sift together flour, baking powder, cinnamon, nutmeg and salt.
5. Mix vanilla, almond, rosewater, lime juice, lime rind and rum and add to dry ingredients.
6. Add mixed fruits.
7. Add browning to desired darkness (always taste browning as some are sometimes salty).
8. Bake for 1 hour or until toothpick comes out clean.
9. Makes two 8 inch cakes.

Note: The wooden spoon should be able to stand up in the batter.

Ingredients for Soaked Fruits

1 lb raisins
1 lb currants
1 lb prunes
Enough White Rum and Red Label Wine to cover fruits when blending

Directions for Soaked Fruits

1. Blend fruits in White Rum and Red Label Wine.
2. Place blended fruits in glass jar.
3. You may need to add rum or wine periodically to keep fruits covered.

Carrot Cake

The carrots add a certain sweetness to the cake along with loads of vitamins and minerals.

Ingredients

2 cups flour
2 cups sugar
2 tsp baking powder
½ tsp baking soda
½ tsp cinnamon
4 beaten eggs
3 cups of finely shredded carrots
½ tsp vanilla
¾ cup cooking oil
½ cup raisins
1 cup walnuts (optional)

Directions

1. Grease and flour two 9 inch round baking pans.
2. Combine flour, sugar, baking powder, baking soda and cinnamon.
3. In another bowl combine eggs, raisins, carrots, vanilla and oil.
4. Add egg mixture to flour mixture.
5. Using a spoon to stir until combined.
6. Pour batter into prepared pans.
7. Bake in a 350°F oven for 30 to 35 minutes or until a toothpick inserted near the center comes out clean.

Note: The carrots need to be finely shredded or they may sink to the bottom of pan during baking.

Pineapple Upside-Down Cake

The cherries in the middle of the pineapple gives this cake a very tasty appearance.

Ingredients

2 tbsp butter
¼ cup brown sugar
1 can pineapple slices
Cherries if desired
1¼ cups flour
1 ½ tsp baking powder

¼ tsp salt
¼ cup shortening
¾ cup sugar
2 eggs beaten
½ cup milk
1 tsp vanilla

Directions

1. Sift flour, baking powder and salt into a bowl.
2. Beat shortening until creamy, add sugar.
3. Add eggs and beat well.
4. Combine vanilla and milk.
5. Add flour and milk mixture alternately stirring until smooth after each addition.
6. Melt butter in a baking pan and sprinkle brown sugar over melted butter.
7. Place pineapple slices over butter mixture.
8. Pour batter over pineapple slices.
9. Bake for 30 minutes at 350°F.
10. Immediately turn upside down onto a serving plate. Let pan remain over cake for a few minutes.
11. Serves 9.

Ginger Cake

This spicy ginger cake is quite a treat. If you love ginger then this is the cake for you.

Ingredients

1¼ cup brown sugar
1 cup butter
4 eggs
¼ cup grated ginger root
1 tsp vanilla
1 cup milk
2½ cups flour
4 tsp baking powder
4 tsp ginger powder
1½ tsp cinnamon
½ tsp salt

Directions

1. Preheat oven to 350°F. Grease and flour 9 inch tin.
2. Cream butter and sugar until light and fluffy.
3. Beat in eggs one at a time then stir in grated ginger and vanilla.
4. In another bowl mix flour, baking powder, ginger, cinnamon and salt.
5. Beat in flour mixture alternately with the milk, until it comes together.
6. Pour into baking pans (makes 2 loaves).
7. Bake for 45 – 50 minutes or until toothpick inserted in center comes out clean.
8. Serves about 10-12.

Mango Cake

There's a saying: "Mango deh bout fi stone dawg." Instead why not make this cake with the extra mangoes.

Ingredients

⅔ cup butter
1 cup sugar
2 eggs
2 cups flour
1 tsp baking soda
½ cup buttermilk
1 tsp vanilla
1 tsp lemon zest
½ cup mango puree
¼ cup mango chunks

Directions

1. Preheat oven to 375°F. Grease and flour baking tin.
2. Cream butter and sugar until light and fluffy.
3. Add eggs and beat well.
4. Mix together flour and baking soda and add to creamed mixture.
5. Fold in buttermilk, vanilla, lemon zest, mango chunks and mango puree.
6. Pour into prepared pan.
7. Bake for 40 to 50 minutes, or until done.

Note: If you don't have buttermilk, you may substitute sour milk. Stir 1 tablespoon of vinegar or lemon juice together with 1 cup of milk and let stand for 10 minutes.

Coffee Cake

If the coffee in the cake wasn't enough add a nice steaming cup of coffee or tea.

Ingredients for Topping

½ cup brown sugar
1 tbsp flour
1 tsp cinnamon
2 tbsp melted butter or margarine

Ingredients for Cake

6 tsp instant coffee crystals
¼ cup oil or melted shortening
1 beaten egg
½ cup milk
1½ cups flour
¾ cup sugar
2 tsp baking powder
½ tsp salt

Directions for Topping

1. Mix brown sugar, flour, cinnamon and melted butter for topping. Set aside.

Directions for Cake

1. Preheat oven to 375°F and grease baking tin
2. Dissolve 4 tsp of coffee crystals in 2 tsp hot water set aside and allow to cool.
3. Combine oil, egg, milk and coffee mixture.
4. Mix dry ingredients (flour, sugar, baking powder, salt and the remaining coffee crystals).
5. Add milk mixture to dry ingredients.
6. Pour into greased baking tin.
7. Sprinkle topping over batter and bake for about 25 minutes or until done.
8. Serve warm.
9. Serves about 10-12.

Pound Cake (Plain Cake)

Great snack with tea or coffee or just plain by itself.

Ingredients

3 cups flour
2 cups sugar
3 tsp baking powder
½ tsp salt
2 cups butter, softened

½ cup milk
1 tsp vanilla
1 tsp almond extract
6 eggs

Directions

1. Preheat oven to 350°F, grease and flour pan.
2. Combine dry ingredients in a large bowl.
3. Add butter, milk, vanilla, and almond extract.
4. Mix on low speed for 1 minute then high speed for 2 minutes. Stop and scrape bowl.
5. Add eggs one at a time mixing well after each addition.
6. Pour batter into prepared baking pan.
7. Bake for 1 hour 15 minutes, or until toothpick inserted in center comes out clean.
8. Cool completely on wire rack.
9. Remove cake from pan.
10. Serves about 10-12.

Banana Bread

This is ideal to make when bananas are plentiful. Gross Mitchell is my favorite.

Ingredients

½ cup butter
1 cup brown sugar
1 egg (beaten)
4 large crushed ripe bananas
2 cups flour
2 tsp baking powder
1 tsp baking soda

1 tsp cinnamon
¼ tsp nutmeg
A pinch of salt
½ cup milk
2 tsp vanilla
¼ tsp grated orange rind
¼ cup raisins

Directions

1. Preheat oven to 350°F. Grease and flour loaf tin.
2. Cream butter and sugar.
3. Add egg to butter and sugar.
4. Add crushed bananas and mix well.
5. Sift flour, baking powder, baking soda, cinnamon, nutmeg and salt.
6. Add flour mixture to butter, sugar and egg mixture along with milk, orange rind and vanilla.
7. Add raisins.
8. Pour into prepared loaf tin.
9. Bake for 1 hour or until toothpick inserted in the center comes out clean.

PUDDINGS

Bread Pudding

Rum is never optional with my famous bread pudding.

Ingredients

2 cups milk
¼ cup margarine (stick) or butter
½ cup sugar
1 tsp cinnamon
1 tsp nutmeg
¼ tsp salt
2 large eggs
8 slices of bread (stale/dry)
½ cup raisins
4 tbsp white rum or whiskey (optional)

Directions

1. Preheat oven to 350°F.
2. Heat milk, sugar, margarine in a saucepan until margarine is melted and then cool.
3. Mix, rum, cinnamon, salt, eggs in a large bowl until well blended.
4. Stir in cubed bread and raisins.
5. Stir in milk mixture. Let sit for 10 - 15 minutes.
6. Pour into an ungreased baking dish.
7. Bake for 40 to 45 minutes until toothpick inserted in center comes out clean.

Note: Letting the mixture rest for 10- 15 minutes allows the raisins and bread to soak.

Sweet Potato Pudding

This is one of Jamaica's traditional desserts. Its not the same as the yams that are used to make sweet potato pie. You need the white sweet potatoes to make this delectable treat.

Ingredients

2 lbs sweet potato (4 to 5 potatoes)
1 cup flour
1 ½ cups brown sugar
1 tsp salt
1 tsp nutmeg
1 tsp cinnamon
2 cups coconut milk
2 tsp vanilla
¼ cup butter (melted)

Directions

1. Preheat oven to 300°F and grease 9 inch baking tin.
2. Peel and grate sweet potatoes.
3. Combine flour, sugar, salt, nutmeg and cinnamon.
4. Combine potatoes, coconut milk, vanilla, melted butter.
5. Combine the dry and the wet ingredients and mix well.
6. Pour into a baking dish.
7. Bake for 45 to 60 minutes or until liquid is absorbed and the top of the pudding is golden brown.

Cornmeal Pudding

This is a perfect treat especially with the goodness on top. My mom makes the best cornmeal pudding.

Ingredients for Pudding

3 cups cornmeal
½ cup flour
¼ tsp salt
½ tsp cinnamon
½ tsp nutmeg
½ cup raisins
2 cans coconut milk
2 cups sugar
1 tsp vanilla
½ cup shredded coconut

Ingredients for Custard

¼ cup coconut milk
2 tbsp sugar
¼ tsp cinnamon
¼ tsp vanilla

Directions

1. Preheat oven to 350°F and grease baking tin.
2. Sift together cornmeal, flour, salt, cinnamon and nutmeg. Then add raisins.
3. Mix coconut milk, sugar, vanilla
4. Combine all ingredients and mix well until there are no lumps.
5. Sprinkle shredded coconut on top.
6. Add pats of butter or margarine to top
7. Bake for 15 minutes or until set.
8. Pour custard mixture on top of pudding.
9. Bake for another 40 – 45 minutes or until set.

TARTS

Plantain Tart

With the signature red dye this treat is just delicious.

Ingredients for Filling

1 lb ripe plantains
1 tbsp margarine
½ cup sugar
½ tsp nutmeg
1 tsp vanilla
2 drops of red food coloring
(to give that signature look)

Ingredients for Crust

2 cups flour
½ tsp salt
1 cup margarine or
shortening
⅓ cup cold water
1 egg (beaten)

Directions for Filling

1. Remove plantains from skin and boil until tender. Drain excess liquid and mash while hot.
2. Add margarine, vanilla, sugar, nutmeg and food coloring and mix well.
3. Let cool until the crust is ready.

Directions for Crust

1. Preheat oven to 350°F.
2. Place flour and salt in bowl and cut shortening into flour mixture with a pastry knife until it looks like bread crumbs.
3. Add cold water as needed and knead until the flour mixture becomes soft and doughy.
4. Flour surface and roll out pastry. Cut into 4 inch circles.
5. Put a teaspoon of plantain filling on each circle.
6. Moisten edge of circle with water. Fold and crimp edges with fork. Prick top of pastry with fork.
7. Beat egg in a bowl and brush the tops of plantain tarts.
8. Bake for about 20 –25 minutes or until golden brown.
9. Allow to cool.
10. Makes 6 plantain tarts.

Note: Pre-made pie crust can be used.

Jamaica's Forgotten Treats | 31

Pineapple Tart

This is one of my favorite tarts growing up as a child.

Ingredients for Filling

1 can crushed pineapple
½ cup sugar (depends on how sweet you want the tarts)
1 tsp vanilla
1 ½ tbsp cornstarch

Ingredients for Crust

2 cups flour
½ tsp salt
1 cup margarine or shortening
⅓ cup cold water
1 egg (beaten)

Directions for Filling

1. Drain most of the liquid from the pineapple in the can, then empty can into a pot, and add vanilla and cornstarch.
2. Add sugar until the desired sweetness is achieved.
3. Boil the pineapple on a medium fire until the juice is absorbed but the fruit is not dry.
4. Stir often to avoid burning. Put aside to cool.

Directions for Crust

1. Preheat oven to 350°F.
2. Place flour and salt in bowl and cut shortening into flour mixture with a pastry knife until it looks like bread crumbs.
3. Add cold water as needed and knead until the flour mixture becomes soft and doughy.
4. Flour surface and roll out pastry. Cut into 4 inch circles.
5. Put a teaspoon of pineapple filling on each circle.
6. Moisten edge of circle with water. Fold and crimp edges with fork. Prick top of pastry with fork.
7. Beat egg in a bowl and brush the tops of pineapple tarts.
8. Bake for about 20 – 25 minutes or until golden brown.
9. Allow to cool.
10. Makes 6 pineapple tarts.

Note: Pre-made pie crust can be used

Cherry Tart

My friend, Ordel, says I cannot write a cookbook without this treat so here goes.

Ingredients for Filling

4-5 cups fresh or frozen unsweetened pitted cherries
1 ½ cup sugar (depends on how sweet you want tarts)
1 tsp vanilla extract
1 tsp lemon juice

Ingredients for Crust

2 cups flour
½ tsp salt
1 cup margarine or shortening
⅓ cup cold water
1 egg (beaten)

Directions for Filling

1. In a small pot stir together cherries, lemon juice and vanilla extract.
2. If using frozen fruit allow fruit to defrost.
3. Add sugar until the desired sweetness is achieved.
4. Boil the cherries on a medium fire until the juice is absorbed but the fruit is not dry.
5. Stir often to avoid burning. Put aside to cool.

Directions for Crust

1. Preheat oven to 350°F.
2. Place flour and salt in bowl and cut shortening into flour mixture with a pastry knife until it looks like bread crumbs.
3. Add cold water as needed and knead until the flour mixture becomes soft and doughy.
4. Flour surface and roll out pastry. Cut into 4 inch circles.
5. Put a teaspoon of cherry filling on each circle.
6. Moisten edge of circle with water. Fold and crimp edges with fork. Prick top of pastry with fork.
7. Beat egg in a bowl and brush the tops of cherry tarts and sprinkle with sugar.
8. Bake for about 20 –25 minutes or until golden brown.
9. Allow to cool.
10. Makes 6 cherry tarts.

Note: Pre-made pie crust can be used.

Appendix

Metric Charts

Dry Measure
¼ tsp = 1 ml
½ tsp = 2 ml
¾ tsp = 4 ml
1 tsp = 5 ml
1 tbsp = 15 ml
2 tbsp = 25 ml
¼ cup = 50 ml
¾ cup = 175 ml
1 cup = 250 ml

Liquid Measure
1 fl oz. (2 tbsp) = 30ml
4 fl ozs. (½ cup) = 125 ml
8 fl ozs. (1 cup) = 250 ml
12 fl ozs. (1 ½ cups) = 375 ml
16 fl ozs. (2 cups) = 500 ml

Equivalent Measures
3 tsp = 1 tbsp
4 tbsp = ¼ cup
5 tbsp + 1 tsp = ⅓ cup
8 tbsp = ½ cup
12 tbsp = ¾ cup
16 tbsp = 1 cup (8ozs)
2 cups = 1 pint (16 ozs)
4 cups = 2 pints = 1 quart (32ozs)
8 cups = 4 pints = ½ gallon = 64 ozs
4 quarts = 1 gallon = 128 ozs

Oven Temperatures
250°F = 120°C
275°F = 140°C
300°F = 150°C
325°F = 160°C
350°F = 180°C
375°F = 190°C
400°F = 200°C
425°F = 220°C
450°F = 230°C

Index

B

Banana Bread   25

Black Cake   17

Bread Pudding   27

Bulla Cake   13

C

Carrot Cake   18

Cherry Tart   33

Coconut Drops   4

Coconut Toto   14

Coffee Cake   23

Cornmeal Pudding   29

D

Duckonoo (Tie Leaf)   8

G

Ginger Cake   20

Gizzada   5

Grater Cake   7

J

Jackass Corn   6

M

Mango Cake   21

P

Peanut Brittle   9

Pineapple Tart   32

Pineapple Upside Down Cake   19

Plantain Tart   31

Pound Cake (Plain Cake)   24

R

Rock Buns   12

S

Spiced Bun (Easter Bun)   11

Sweet Potato Pudding   28